THE TITHE AND ITS ANOINTING

G. EMERSON SCOTT

authorHOUSE®

AuthorHouse™
1663 Liberty Drive
Bloomington, IN 47403
www.authorhouse.com
Phone: 1-800-839-8640

First published by AuthorHouse 8/19/2009

ISBN: 978-1-4389-8792-7 (sc)

Printed in the United States of America
Bloomington, Indiana

This book is printed on acid-free paper.

The order of the Lord for the lives of his people has remained consistent and constant from generation to generation. How God deals with his people, what He expects of them, how He rewards them and visits them, etc…, establishes for us the pattern of God. Whenever God responds to man, He looks for His pattern. The glory of the Lord will only be present where the pattern can be found. The pattern reminds God of himself and His promises to his people.

The tithe, the tenth of the increase, is a pattern that God honors. The honoring of this pattern releases the glory of the Lord in the form of supernatural increase, and an accounting of the ten percent as if God had been given the whole.

The use of tithes is not only seen in biblical history, but in secular history as well. Though most like to ascribe tithing to the Law given to Israel, it was a practice long before then. Abram presented the tenth of the spoils of his victory to Melchizedek in Genesis 14:20. Jacob, after his vision at Luz, devoted a tenth of all his property to God in Genesis 28:22.

This biblical practice, which became a law in the book of Leviticus, is yet in the twenty-first century a divine pattern that God honors. Bishop G. Emerson Scott has been blessed to receive an awesome revelation of the tithe and how we should relate to it today. After you read what he has to say, you may ask if perhaps the reason many cannot break out of their financial dilemma may be due to not just how the people tithe, but how the priests (spiritual leaders) tithe.

I commend the courage that Scott has to put this in print. Money is yet seen as a taboo when discussed in the religious community, though in every other culture, it is seen as a necessity. Frequently, spiritual leaders will acquiesce when it come to discussing tithes, offerings, and financial giving. Yet, we must all confess that money is no less a need for the religious community then it is for any other community. I challenge you to read further. See what Scott has to say. If you are a preacher or teacher, he gives you some great information and instructions to draw on. If you are a skeptic, prepare to be challenged in your belief. If you are a non-giver, you may be convinced that tithing is a "GREAT INVESTMENT". It pays great dividends when it is done in accordance to the pattern of God.

Be blessed as you keep reading.
Bishop Ralph L. Dennis, PH.D.
Senior Pastor
Kingdom Worship Center

Table of Contents

Preface

This book is authored for the purpose of transforming the minds and lives of God's people, that we might have the pattern of God for His revealed glory. Like Abraham to Israel, I want to be to this generation of believers, who need to see a present life of one who follows the pattern of Tithe and Offerings and its benefits.

This is a real issue to me and not just a studied issue. Since I was twelve years of age, I tithed and have **_always_** lived in the **FAVOR OF GOD,** even in times when the masses were in financial struggles.

So read and swallow for the manifestation!

Acknowledgments

God, our Father who has blessed the work that He has placed in my hands.

To all of my sons and daughters of Trinity Fellowship Church - where I reside as senior pastor and founder in Houston, Texas.

A special thanks to TFC Administrative Staff; and Power of God Ministries – my personal preaching and teaching ministry.

THE DEVIL IS DEFEATED AND GOD GETS ALL THE GLORY!

Chapter 1

The Tithe In The Old Testament

"For whatever things were written before were written for our learning, that we through the patience and comfort of the scriptures might have hope" – Romans 15:4

In his letter to the Romans, a verse of which appears in the epigraph above, Paul reminds us that what was written has been written for us as a pattern. This passage indicates a writing we are to use as a reference.

What has been written for us? What was written for us is the Old Testament where God laid out patterns for his people. I cannot ignore the Old Testament and say that I don't need the Old Testament. The Old Testament establishes patterns, instructions, and rules for me, and anointing comes with it. With every pattern, there is an anointing. With every word that was written before that was for our learning, there is an anointing. The anointing is in the instructions. Patterns carry with them anointing.

I had the benefit of listening to Dr. Creflo Dollar in Atlanta, and I received a burden in my spirit to teach on the three areas of giving and the anointing that comes with them. If we are going to view the Old Testament, we have to look at two of the people that God speaks about for these areas of giving. We have to know the distinction between the Levites and the priests.

Of the three words in Israel's priesthood, the Levites happen to be the lowest. Israel priest and temple personal were chosen from the first born of every tribe. Every time there was a first born in the camp of Israel, he was committed to the Levitical priesthood. God later changed this and decided that he would not use the first born because the first-born did not have the courage or the heart to be Levites. Therefore, he chose one of the tribes of Israel to do everything that the Levites were supposed to do. That tribe was the tribe of Levi. The tribe of Levi was the only tribe that stood with Moses when the children of Israel decided they wanted to worship the golden calf.

God brought them to a place of change, for many of them who were already Levites walked away from that to which they are called. Exodus 32:25-39 and Numbers 3:11-13 reads: *"Then the Lord spoke to Moses saying, "Now behold I myself have taken the Levites from among the children of Israel instead of every first-born who opens the womb among the children of Israel. Therefore, the Levites shall be mine because all the first-born are mine. On the day that I struck, all the first-born in the land of Egypt, I sanctified to myself all of the first-born in Israel, both man and beast. They shall be mine: I am the Lord.* " He spoke to Moses saying, *"I myself have taken unto myself."*

The first-born used to be the Levites, but God got angry with them: Exodus 32:25-29 reads: *"Now when Moses saw that the people were unrestrained (for Aaron had restrained them, to their shame among their enemies), then Moses stood at the entrance of the camp and said, Whoever is on the Lord's side – come to me! And all the sons of Levi gathered themselves together to him. And he said to them...Let every man put his sword on his side, and go in and out from entrance to entrance throughout the camp, and let every man kill his brother, every man his companion, and every man his neighbor. So the sons of Levi did according to the word of Moses. And about three thousand men of the people fell that day. Then Moses said, consecrate yourselves today to the Lord that he may bestow on you a blessing this day, for every man has opposed his son and his brother."*

What happened is that they became worshippers with Aaron when they built the golden calf while Moses was on Mt. Sinai praying, God was angry with them. When Moses came back down to call order, the only people who stood with him were the tribe of Levi. So God says, "Now, I'm not taking the first-born anymore; the only people that are going to serve as Levites are the tribes of Levi." **Why?** They were the ones who stood with the man of God to oppose everyone who stood against the Son of God. Levites are not priests they are the ones who care for the temple of God; they are the ones who do the work.

The employees of this church are considered Levites. The minute one opposes the vision of God against me, I fire them. I am not a Levite I am a priest. If nobody stands with me, the Levites should. Anytime I go to do anything, the Levites had better go before me. There is nothing that God calls me too or to do that the Levites should be the last ones doing it. The only ones God will take are those who will stand with the Son of God and for his Son. They are the only ones who are qualified to be Levites. They benefit from the Tithes of the people. The people of the congregation pay Levites and are due respect.

God chose the Levites as those who stood with the vision. God had become angry at the Levites because they had become comfortable with what they were paid. They were no more than God robbers. If you will only stand as long as you get paid, you are a hireling and you will not protect the sheep. Now, there is a reason I was able to turn to this subject. If the workers of the church are out of order, they affect the anointing of the offering. There needs to be excellence in the church, but it must be paid for. We want to claim how incompetent people are, but we want to nickel and dime.

Understand who they are. Number 18:24-32 reads, *"For the tithes of the children of Israel which they offer up as a heave offering to the Lord, I have given to the Levites as an inheritance; therefore I have said to them, among the children of Israel they shall have no inheritance."* They have no inheritance; therefore, they get your tithe.

Who are the tithes for? They are for the Levites, not the priest. It says, *"then the Lord said to Moses saying, Speak thus to the Levites and say to them, when you take from the children of Israel the tithes which I have given you from them as an inheritance then you* *shall offer up a heave offering of it to the Lord a tenth of the tithe."* Levites are to give a "heave" offering, a tenth. Verse 27 explains, *"And your heave of offering shall be reckoned to you as though it were the grain of the threshing floor and as the fullness of the winepress."* God said he is going to consider your tithe equal to the fullness of the winepress. God is treating the holiness of the tithe, the holiness of the gift as holy. God says he will reckon it as though it were the grain of the threshing floor and as the fullness of the winepress. The whole of the tithe gift is holy. God explains in verse 28 that, *Thus you shall also offer a heave offering to the Lord from all you tithes which you receive from the children of Israel, and you shall give the Lord's heave offering from it to Aaron the priest."*

Every Levite is to tithe and also give a heave offering to the priest. Anybody working with me not only gives to the church but also gives a heave offering to me. Anybody who works for the church must give a tithe and an offering to the priest from the best part. If you tithe fifty dollars ($50.00) but your heave offering to the priest is two dollars ($2.00) and/or five dollars ($5.00) that is not right. You must give the best of it. Lets look at why you should give your best.

As you give to the priest, you tap into the anointing of the fullness of the priest. The priest receives the remaining offering after all of the needs of the house have been addressed. When the priest began to eat of the fat, it trickles down like anointing oil and allows the giver to tap into the anointing of the priest. This guarantees whatever you *think,* you might be short to have surplus in; you are tapping into a return.

The tithe of the rest of the nation was to provide for the needs of the Levites. The nation's tithe takes care of the church workers. The tithe cannot build churches. The tithe takes care of the lights and air conditioning. How many of you would have taken the job you work on if there were no benefits? Most would not. What most people do is force the Levites in this house to work without benefits, something you would not accept. They force them to live without benefits when they will not tithe. This causes them to be cursed. There is a curse that exists in the house because the people do not tithe. The tithe goes to provide for the needs of the Levites. If we want to build a church, that comes from the offerings.

See verse 30: *"Therefore you shall say to them: When you have lifted up the best of it, then the rest shall be accounted to the Levites as the produce of the threshing floor and as the produce of the winepress."* Who are they talking about? They are talking to the offering. Levites should talk to their money. Verses 31 and 32 read, *"You may eat it in any place, you and your households, for it is your reward for your work in the tabernacle of meeting. And you shall bear no sin because of it, when you have lifted up the best of it. But you shall not profane the holy gifts of the children of Israel, lest you die."* Levites are not wrong for being taken care of.

If you are a curse to what we give you, then you curse us and die. Do not take what the people pay you, or buy a hotel room for somebody else. You curse the people when you do. You curse our gifts and the people when you take what is given and go toward ungodly pleasures.

Why is there a curse? Numbers 3:5-9 reads: *"And the Lord spoke to Moses saying: Bring the tribe of Levi near, and present them before Aaron the priest, that they may serve him and they shall attend to his needs and the needs of the whole congregation before the tabernacle of meeting to do the work of the tabernacle. Also, they shall attend to all the furnishings of the tabernacle of meeting and to the needs of the children of Israel to do the work of the tabernacle. And you shall give the Levites to Aaron and his sons; they are given entirely to him from among the children of Israel."*

Levites of this church not only work for the church but also are the priest's. There are other Levites that are not paid through the church. Why? These Levites take care of the priest's needs. Numbers 16:9 says, *"Is it a small thing to you that the God of Israel has separated you from the congregation of Israel, to bring you near to Himself, to do the work of the tabernacle of the Lord, and to stand before the congregation to serve them."* He has separated the Levite from the congregation to bring them near to himself; if anybody is consecrated, you – the Levites – are. Not just because you hold the offering and their gifts that are holy, but you could curse us all, because you are to be consecrated to him. If anyone in the congregation is to be holy, you are. If anybody should set an example, you should. Everybody wants to read the book of Timothy and say, *"The preacher must be blameless."* You too must be blameless. There is a certain character and integrity that belongs to you as Levites, and if you cannot handle it, then get out of leadership.

How can you reflect me as your priest when you are in a pair of shorts, flip-flops, and a t-shirt in church? There is a certain order that you are to follow; otherwise, you bring a curse on the whole congregation. A certain anointing belongs to you and a certain consecration goes with you because a certain part of the gifts of the people of God goes to you. You are not just a musician. If I asked you to do something besides play, you would probably have a fit because you do not get paid to do anything else. You are a Levite, and your job is to take care of the priest. To do anything less is to curse everybody in the congregation. No one needs a curse on his or her money. We have too many things to deal with than to be dealing with curses. Get yourself together because you are taken care of by the tithe. There is a certain anointing that belongs in the house of God because of you. Any affairs of your life that are out of order get them in order. There is a certain anointing that belongs in the house of God, and you are a part of it. The first portion of the gifts that come forth from the people of God goes to you as a Levite.

When you come to church, you are not larger than life. There is only one large person here and that is the priest. He is not even large; God is the only one large in here. I am tired of cursed people hanging on me, sucking me dry, and preventing my vision from coming to pass. I love everybody, but it is time to rise.

Because of the work of the Levites, the holiness of the temple was maintained. During David's reign, the Levites were integrated into the administration of the government. They became the administration. They took care of the music, tables, priests, and everything in the tabernacle. They were responsible for taking it apart and putting it together. They put everything in its place. They became the government of Israel. They became judges and treasurers. You are not in a dead-end job as a Levite. You can always be promoted. I don't ever want to talk to a Levite and ask, "I want you to come and work for the church five days a week" and you say, "no, that's not the direction I'm moving in." Get out, you don't have my back in war.

Church, you need to bring a level of accountability to the Levites. The praise leader is a Levite because the leader leads the congregation into worship. You need to do better by your Levites, and the only way to do better is to tithe. Your Levites are underpaid and overworked. I look at other ministries and wonder why they can get people with the degrees and the skill, but I cannot pay for people with those skills. Yet you say, "I'm tired of mediocre ministry", yet we don't get cheap until we get to the house of God. You don't tithe.

Something got into my spirit that needs to happen. We need to become a church that is made up of one hundred percent (100%) tithers. We don't want curses from the body, Levite, priest, or congregation. The first order of God in the three areas of giving that have an anointing upon them is in the area of tithe, and they go to the Levites. Pastors cannot hire the people they need to bring vision to pass without it. In Corinthians, there is no need in boasting in anybody else's labor, everything God has for us can be done, but we have got to change our mind-set.

I Chronicles 9:22 reads: *"All those chosen as gatekeepers were two hundred and twelve. They were recorded by their genealogy, in the villages. David and Samuel the seer had appointed them to their trusted office."* This is a pattern; the gatekeepers of the house were also Levites, parking lot people. Whatever was appointed to them was for them and their children. There is no way to operate in the pattern of God, and it does not affect generations. Verse 23 reads: *"So they and their children were in charge of the gates of the house of the Lord, the house of the tabernacle, by assignment."* This is a pattern for ministry. The four chiefs at the gates were Levites.

To do a level of ministry that is the call of the Kingdom of God, you must have a system of accountability for people to bring things to pass. You cannot do it being cheap. "I think I want steak tonight, but I only want to pay ninety-nine cents." Well, tacos are all you get. "…and they lodged all around the house of God because they had the responsibility and they were in charge of opening it every morning." There is an anointing in following the pattern of God. The first order of God is caring for the priest and the Levites. The Levites are cared for by the tithe, and it is a tenth of your increase. You do not expect to do ministry above what is done in the house with the tithe.

God has three areas of offering: Tithe, offering and first fruit. Tithe goes to the Levite; offering goes to the work of ministry and the building of the kingdom of God. First fruit goes to the priest. Caring for the poor is not benevolence, it is doing ministry. We build and expand ministry by our offerings for the poor. To God it is treachery and an abomination. You are opposing to His order to His face.

God says to bring the tithe for the Levites and take care of them and then the windows of heaven will be open for you. We have been going too long doing things without integrity, and we have been doing things expecting too much, but not doing much. That has to be turned around. This teaching is turning it around. Everybody should want to work for the church.

"Nobody takes care of you like the church." This is what I would like to hear Levites say.

Chapter 2

FOLLOWING THE OLD TESTAMENT PATTERN OF GIVING

"And it shall be when the LORD shall bring thee into the land of the Canaanites, so he swear into thee and to thy fathers, and shall give it thee,

That thou shalt set apart unto the LORD all that openeth the matrix, and every firstling that cometh of a beast, which thou hast; the males shall be the Lord's.

And every firstling of an ass thou shalt redeem with a lamb; and if thou wilt not redeem it, then thou shalt break his neck; and all the firstborn of man among thy children shalt thou redeem." Exodus 13:11-13

I am amazed when I listen to the radio, which I don't do much, at the foolishness of what I hear. Recently, I heard a man preaching that we need to repent for women preachers and women pastors, which he was saying, was not ordained. I am amazed that people do not think we should examine the Old Testament. The New Testament tells you what comes to pass as a result of doing the *"how"* of the Old Testament.

As the epigraph to this chapter indicates, hope is the manifestation of the things in the scripture. So then, I have to examine patterns that were written in the past so that I have what the scripture says. There are certain things that are manifest, and I have got to consider the things that are written as patterns.

The Levites of the ministry are the people who work in the ministry to make things happen. The bible declares that the tithe goes to the Levite. That is everyone who works for things to happen in ministry, which is your janitor, financial officer, secretary, but not your pastor. These are the people who serve the sanctuary of God on a daily basis.

If we follow the pattern of the Old Testament, the men who serve as servants in the sanctuary would be Levites and would be getting paid for what they do. We must recognize that the call of ministry and excellence that goes with it will cost something. You cannot expect excellence and keep the people who work hungry. If anybody is going to do well, it ought to be those who work for God.

The Levites are the lowest of three orders in the priesthood of Israel: the Levites are those who are assistants to the priests. There are three areas of giving: one to the Levites; one to the priests; and one to the high priest. We recognize in today's time three offerings, but we only really recognize two: tithe and offering. Now, the third one that you operate in is called a "Love Offering". That is equivalent to first fruit. The way we operate, a love offering is out of a pattern according to the word of God. There is anointing that goes with each one that benefits the ones who release it. We want to examine these offerings and God's order for each so that the pattern of God releases to us what the scripture says we should have as a result of doing them.

Let us examine the definition of the word "*wealth*". Train your mind to understand that wealth does not mean money. The bible is very clear in making a distinction between wealth and riches. Wealth is knowledge, ability, and power. God says, "I have given you the power to get wealth". In essence, He has given you the ability to get wealth – knowledge, ability, and power. He has given us access to ability.

"*Riches*" is a word we have to keep in mind. We want wealth and riches, not just wealth and not just riches. Riches without wealth can be destructive. Riches without wealth can mess you up. Money without knowledge, character and discipline can mess you up. Money magnifies whatever you are when you are broke, you are just a bigger one of those when you get money, unless a change takes place. The problem is not that God hasn't blessed us with money. We just did not have wealth at the time we got it.

When you look back over your life, there are some things you cannot have again because your stuff is too messed up. You want to get to the place that anything you let go is something you released and you are able to be a blessing in other people's lives.

When you are dealing with the priests, remember that they were originally the firstborn in families. In Exodus 23:11-13, God chose the tribe of Levi when Moses went up against the worshippers of the golden altar. The tribe of Levi was the only tribe that stood to maintain the order of God. It pleased God, so he stopped using the firstborn and started using the tribe of Levi (Numbers 3:11-13; Exodus 32:25-39; Deuteronomy 10:6-9).

After choosing the tribe of Levi, the Lord chose to change the order of the tithe so that it would come from every nation to take care of the Levites because they were consumed with taking care of the tabernacle (Numbers 18:24-32). The duty of the Levite was always to the priest, whether a psalmist, financial officer, or gatekeeper. Whatever role Levites played, they were in assistance to the priest. No Levites should function to make sure it is accomplished. Their job is to assist the priest to release him to God to minister. Solomon made sure the Levites were in their places (Numbers 3:5-9) as the temple was built; he read and implemented the instructions left by his father.

In I Chronicles 9:22-28, we find the different duties that were under the order of the Levites. Also, we recognize that God eventually moved the administration or the government of the nation under the Levites. There should be some administrative skills in the ranks of the Levites. When a ministry grows, it does not mean that the money grows; it usually works that the more people in attendance, the offering increases very little in proportion to ministry. If there are more members, the number of people being responsible and accountable to the order of God will increase. Your challenges in relation to money can be addressed if you are giving changes. There is anointing of increase that comes with the order of God. God never said the tithe would usher in the anointing for debt cancellation; the anointing is on first fruit. The anointing for surplus is on offering. The anointing that is on tithe is an anointing for increase. It is where God enables you to overcome obstacles that are unseen. The anointing on the tithe is to take care of the unseen. The anointing on first fruit brings about debt cancellation.

Numbers 6 of the Old Testament is where we begin. Numbers 6:22-27 reads, *"And the Lord spoke unto Moses, saying, Speak to Aaron and his sons, saying, This is the way you shall bless the children of Israel* (that is you, the congregation of people). *Say to them, "The Lord bless thee and keep thee, the Lord make His face shine upon you and be gracious unto you; the Lord lift up His countenance upon you, and give you peace. So they shall put My name on the children of Israel, and I will bless them."*

The job of the priest is obviously not in caring for the tabernacle that is for the Levite. There is a job for everybody, and there is an anointing that goes with it. The Levites' job is to care for ministry; they are to care for the tabernacle. The priest's job is to bless the people.

Exodus 28:29 is for pattern: *"So Aaron shall bear the names of the sons of Israel in the breastplate of judgment over his heart, when he goes into the holy place, as a memorial before the Lord continually."* Where are the people of God to rest? They are to rest in the heart of the priest. It is hard to keep the people in the heart of the priest when the priest is entangled with the affairs of the tabernacle. Solomon was not entangled in the affairs of building the temple. He simply read the orders to the people. Many times we lay too much responsibility on the heart of the priest when we do not take up the areas of responsibility that belong to us. If we do not take care of our areas of responsibility, our own blessings are cut off. The priest should be kept free to bless the people and keep them in his heart. You have no idea the amount of days that I think about you, only my wife knows or my armor bearers. I will say to my wife, "so and so is coming to my mind, something is wrong with him", she will say, "I was thinking about that too."

Exodus 28:30 reads: *"And you shall put in the breastplate of judgment the Urim and the Thummim, and they shall be over Aaron's heart when he goes in before the Lord. So Aaron shall bear the judgment of the children of Israel over his heart before the Lord continually."* He is either blessing the people or interceding for them, but he is not involved in the government that takes care of the tabernacle.

Deuteronomy 31:7-9 reads, *"And Moses called Joshua and said to him in the sight of all Israel, Be strong and of good courage, for you must go with this people to the land which the Lord has sworn to their fathers to give them, and you shall cause them to inherit it. And the Lord, He is the One who goes before you. He will be with you; He will not leave you nor forsake you; do not fear nor be dismayed."* What is He doing? Impartation! Moses does not make it into the land of promise, so he imparted what he cannot finish and/or do in the lives of people who are. One of the things you need to learn is to see yourself in ministry as an extension of your priest, and allow him to make impartations on your life.

Some of you do not want to be close to the preacher. You want to come to church, go home, and that is it. The priest is wearing the garments that God has given him in order to make impartations. It is a fact that people who stay close to me are people whose lives are affected and it should not be that way. Anybody who rests in the garment of the priest should receive the impartation of the priest.

Old Testament is pattern; New Testament is manifestation. II Corinthians 10:12-13 tells us: ***"For we dare not class ourselves or compare ourselves with those commend themselves. But they, measuring themselves among themselves, are not wise. We, however, will not boast beyond measure, but within the limits of the sphere, which God appointed us – a dimension, sphere, or place that God has appointed to the priest, and it includes you.***

Every rise that God gives to your priest should be evident also in your life, but only if you receive the impartation. ***"For we dare not class ourselves or compare ourselves with those who commend themselves,"*** the Bible tells us. If everything that operates under this anointing was all about me, so that it was all for me, it would not be wise. Why? Old Testament pattern says the only inheritance I have is in you; which means nothing happens for me if it does not happen for you. If you do not get your inheritance, I do not get mine.

If there is a sphere that God calls me to, its one that includes you, but if nothing happens for you, then nothing happens for me. ***"We, however,"*** the Bible says, ***"will not boast beyond measure, but within the limits of the sphere…"*** which especially includes you. How many times did he say *especially*? He said it twice. There is a sphere in which anointing the priest operates and it includes you. Only a fool does not want to see his priest free. If the priest cannot be free, the people will not be free.

If the priest's life does not change ("Reverend", some might say, you're just not like you used to be".) then there will be no way to effect change in you and call you to a level of accountability. II Corinthians 10:7-8 records that there is an anointing that rests in the garments of the priest and his job is to make impartations in the people to go where he cannot go, do what he cannot do, and reach into areas he cannot reach. Examples of this can be seen with Moses and his being denied entry to the Promised Land. Every priest has to function in the tabernacle, but he does not function in the tabernacle. He functions through the Levites. The priest's assignment is to make impartation into the lives of the people so that they are able to go into spiritual dimensions and function for the power of the Kingdom of God. I have got to make impartation upon leaders, upon men, and upon women. I have to make impartation to the educated. I have got to inspire someone to become our next mayor, councilman, or our next congressman. I cannot go into these spheres. My sphere of influence includes you, so wherever your influence is, that is where mine is.

Some of you would be angry if I called you on your job and said, "This is what I need you to do for me." You would say, "See, he did not talk to me before he needed something." Deuteronomy 31:9-11 declares, ***"So Moses wrote this law and delivered it to the priests, and the sons of Levi, who bore the Ark of the Covenant of the Lord, and to all the elders of Israel.***

And Moses commanded them, saying: At the end of every seven years, at the appointed time in the year of release, at the Feast of Tabernacles, when all Israel comes to appear before the Lord your God in this place which He chooses, you shall read this law before all Israel in their hearing." What is one of his other assignments? One of his other assignments is to bring instruction into the life of the people.

One of the assignments of the priest is to bring the order of God into your life. We want him to do everything. The old school said the pastor had to be the one to dedicate the babies, perform baptisms, and serve communion, but you do not see that in the New Testament. First of all, you very seldom see the word pastor. Understand that there was an order of priests established. If I have Levites assigned to the tabernacle, then there are jobs that can be assigned to them or other pastors assigned to do it. But you say, "If my pastor does not do it, it is not right." Well, like Envogue says, "Free your mind and the rest will follow".

It may be the wrong song but at any rate, part of the assignment of the priest besides making impartation, blessing the people, and keeping them in his heart is to also bring them the instruction of the law or challenge. Part of my assignment is to bring challenge into your life. I want to push you to explore areas you otherwise would not explore. There are some things you need to be pushed in.

If God brings you every message you like to hear, you would remain lazy. God has to challenge you to do things you do not want to do. It is the priest's job to bring challenge into the life of the people of God. There is not one time he is the gatekeeper. Not one time is he the worship leader. This means that if the care of the tabernacle is going to happen so that ministry is not delayed while the priest is worrying about light bulbs or having the grass cut, then somebody else has to be hired to care for the tabernacle. If you are going to increase Levites, the tithe has to be increased. Now, you cannot go to somebody else's ministry and say, "This is the kind of ministry I like." You are resting in somebody else's labor and that body of people is taking care of their Levites. You should take on your portion of the burden in the tithe no matter where you are. Something happens when you take care of the Levites.

In the writing and in Elijah's life, he called for the tithe. There was so much that the priests and Levites began to share it until the congregation who brought it also got blessed. If you only put $2.50 in your gas tank, you are not going very far, especially these days. Just cranking the car to start it will deplete the fuel. If you want to take journeys faster and longer, it takes more gas. There must be an increase in giving so that ministry increases. Do not talk about what you would like to see but fail to invest the finances. Every person has to become responsible in bringing the tithe. Tithes take care of the people (who labor in ministry – staff), and offerings build the church. Most of us, through a conviction in our hearts, have been convinced to tithe, but we do not give an offering. Malachi says, **"Bring your tithe and offering"** (see Malachi 3:7-12).

Each person has a function in giving and in that function is order to take care of the people. You know Malachi 3 without looking at it or maybe you heard it but do not know it. We are not going to ask, *"Will a man rob God?"* We already know he will, so we do not have to read that verse. In verse 10 we are commanded, *"Bring ye all the tithes into the storehouse,"* God says, *"that there may be meat in mine house."* It is a matter of sufficiency and efficiency (all that is required to suffice). What must be met in ministry are the needs of people. The people who meet the needs of the people in the house will be the Levites. Their ministry will go forth to the people of the church who provide for the needs of ministry leaders (Levites) who will, in turn, take care of their needs and also take care of the tabernacle. The purpose of the tithe is not to satisfy you. The purpose of the tithe is to supply meat in the house, so that whatever needs there are, they are met.

The New Testament in the Book of Acts records, *"When the people of God came together after the Pentecost and everybody sold the things that they had so that all things could have all things in common."* The needs of the people were met: *"That there may be meat in mine house, and prove me now herewith, saith the Lord of hosts, if I will not open you the windows of heaven, and pour you out a blessing."* You cannot be a blessing in the house, meeting the needs of other people, without God blessing you; you open yourself for the blessing.

In Malachi 3:10, God tells us, *"If I will not open you the windows of heaven, and pour you out a blessing, that there shall not be room enough to receive it."* The anointing on tithe is that of more than enough. He is not talking about your needs. He is just talking about a blessing, saying, *"If you bring me the tithe, I will bless you so that there will not be room enough to receive it all."* Now, is God a wasteful God? Does he give things so that they are wasted? If God does not release to the point that it spoils, what does he mean then when he says not having room enough to receive it? The anointing on tithe is that a surplus is created for which no needs yet exist.

I bring the Lord the tithe to take care of the needs of people so there is meat in the house. God prepares a surplus that I don't have a need for yet. Now you say, "Pastor, I have some needs. Why aren't my needs being met?" If you have needs that are not being met and you are tithing, you need to talk to the people who are not tithing. You should have a surplus. The people who are not tithing are not releasing into your needs. They are getting blessed and your stuff is getting held up. There is an anointing on tithe, and it requires that every man and woman must come out of a place of selfishness and release into the needs of others so that the meat in the house of God can be supplied to every need. Not only in the natural, but if God has to give you things that there will not be room enough to receive. There are some things that are not going to be released in the natural that are still reserved in the heavens that have not made it to the natural yet. You need to talk to the people who are holding it up. That is why it is important that everybody tithe.

I began confessing that my church members become one hundred percent tithers for the life of everybody in the house of God and for the needs of people we have yet to meet.

You say, "Pastor, money is so tight I can not tithe." That's why you need to. Here is the anointing for it. He says, *"And I will rebuke the devourer for your sakes, and he shall not destroy the fruit of your ground."* You can quote it; you just will not do it. He did not say he may not but he says, *"You bring the tithe and I will rebuke the devourer so that he will not destroy the ground."* Some of you have destroyed fruit and ground. It is not to uphold God in what he is saying, but to convict you so that you can do what God has commanded.

God said something to me about delays: "No more delays." He told me to open to a certain place in the Bible. I actually saw it in my sleep and then turned to it: "No more delays." It was connected to a word he gave me the day before. It was in another chapter in another book. I am hearing God saying, "The things of God exist in the heavens, but they do not work in your life until you know it." There are principles and powers that God has given you that do not work in your life until you know them. There are certain powers in your life that do not work until you know them. There is potential in your life that does not work until you wake it up. When God spoke that word in me, I promise you, every time I ran into a delay, my mind clicked back to God saying, "No more delays." When I commanded it, it happened.

I was on a plane coming home, and the pilot said, "There are eight planes in front of us waiting to land on the runway, and we are number nine in line." I had to be somewhere shortly, and I needed to get in my car to get there. I said, "Father," and then I said, "I am sorry, I was about to bother you, Father." I then said, "I command there will be no more delays." The minute I said, "I command no more delays," the pilot immediately came back over the intercom and said, "Everything is clear."

God says, *"The devourer will not destroy your ground or your fruit."* You must command that the ground and fruit be safe, command any foul demon that puts his hand on your fruit to be released. God says, *"The devourer…shall not destroy the fruits of your ground; neither shall your vine cast her fruit before the time in the field, saith the Lord…all nations shall call you blessed, for ye shall be a delightsome land."* God is talking about the vine of descendents not casting the fruit before its time. There is an anointing on tithe, it is not only the release of God to command that the enemy leave my stuff alone, but also I am feeding into the generations after me. That is what ministry should do, anyway; it should affect generations after me. God is going to protect your children, and nothing in them will come before its time. What does the enemy want to do with every plan of God? The enemy wants to kill it, but God is saying that nothing is going to miss its purpose. There is an anointing on the tithe for the security of our families.

We are not talking about the increase, but things you have sown, naturally. It is not the increase that is over and above what you sowed. We are just talking about what you put there. If you understand sowing and reaping, you never reap what you sow; you always reap more than you sow. We are just talking about the things you planted.

God says, "There is an anointing for it and the anointing that is on the ground is something you can command and it is for the generations behind you, also." Malachi records, ***"And all nations shall call you blessed, for ye shall be a delightsome land."*** There is a glory that should be on your life that makes people recognize the profitableness of serving your God.

My mother was a cosmetologist for over thirty-something years. Most of the money that came into our house came from her. My daddy pastored a church, and his salary was one hundred twenty-five dollars a week. Some Sundays there was not enough for that. He tithed like he had it, and my mother tithed. There was one thing that people always concluded about my family and that was, we were rich.

Right now, people think I'm loaded, and I do not tell them any different. When you look at me, I ought to be delightsome. The look about my countenance makes people say, "Doc, I just want to be like you." I used to say, "No, you do not want that." But now I say, "Yeah, you will get there, your time is coming." I realize that whatever they see I cannot deny because it is not mine to deny. There is a glory that is on my life that comes from responding to the pattern of God. If it is visible, it is because there is a spirit that exists, and, if so the manifestation is not far behind.

First of all, that anointing is again impartation, and it comes from your not taking care of the preacher, but just taking care of the Levites in the house. I am not saying, "Take care of the preacher, and your stuff will be taken care of." This anointing comes from taking care of the people who work for the church. There is an anointing that comes with it, not because you gave sacrificially, but just because you are following the pattern of God and taking care of the people who take care of God's business.

If people are not tithing because of fear or because money is too tight to do it, they need to be released from that. Everyone has got to tithe. Get the tapes on ***"Beware the Locusts"***. Trust me; something is always going to come up. There is a discipline that has to come in your life in order to release God so that you can stop being messed up so regularly.

Chapter 3

THE TRUE MEANING OF THE LEVITE

"And all the tithe of the land, whether of the seed of the land, or of the fruit of the tree, is the Lord's; it is holy unto the Lord." Leviticus 27:30

The caring for the Levite and the order of God for the Levite comes through the tithe, the first fruit. The first mention of the tithe is in Genesis 14:17. Let us begin at Genesis 14:13: *"Then one who had escaped came and told Abram the Hebrew, for he dwelt by the terebinth trees of Mamre the Amorite, brother of Eshcol and brother of Aner; and they were allies with Abram. Now when Abram heard that his brother was taken captive, he armed his three hundred and eighteen trained servants who were born in his own house, and went in pursuit as far as Dan. He divided his forces against them by night and he and his servants attacked them and pursued them as far as Hobah, which is north of Damascus. So he brought back all the goods, and also brought back his brother Lot and his goods, as well as the women and the people. And the king of Sodom went out to meet him at the Valley of Shaveh (that is, the King's Valley), after his return from the defeat of Chedorlaomer and the kings who were with him. The Melchizedek king of Salem brought out bread and wine; he was the priest of God Most High. And he blessed him and said, blessed be Abram of God Most High, possessor of heaven and earth; and blessed be God Most High, who has delivered your enemies into your hand and he gave him a tithe of all. Now the king of Sodom said to Abram, give me the persons and take the goods for yourself. But Abram said to the king of Sodom, I have raised my hand to the Lord, God Most High, and the Possessor of heaven and earth, that I will take nothing from a thread to a sandal strap, and that I will not take anything that is yours, lest you should say, "I have made Abram rich."* Most people overlook verse 21.

Is not the tithe a tenth of all you possess? It's a tenth of your possessions. Abram gives him the tenth of all of the goods that he took. Melchizedek says, "I don't want the goods, just give me the persons."

"But Abram said to the king of Sodom, I have raised my hand to the Lord, God Most High, the Possessor of heaven and earth, that I will take nothing, from a thread to a sandal strap, and that I will not take anything that is yours, lest you should say, "I have made Abram rich...except only what the young men have eaten, and the portion of the men who went with me...let them take their portion."

Chapter 15 follows: ***"After these things the Word of the Lord came to Abram in a vision, saying, do not be afraid, Abram, I am your shield, your exceedingly great reward."*** I am looking for the anointing from the tithe I honor the Lord with. I am looking for the anointing that comes with the tithe. The first mention always establishes pattern. Abram gives the tithe, but he is not thinking about himself and that's his heart. I am looking for the pattern and the anointing. The tragedy with most of us is that when we give tithe, we think of us, and, in fact, when we do not tithe, we think of us.

When the King of Sodom said, "Give me the persons and you take the goods," Abram said, "No." If you are going to follow the pattern of this type of release of resources and the possessions you have, the first thing you need to do is get you out of the picture. As long as you are in the picture, you will always have a reason not to honor God.

The first lesson says, "Forget about you." You take yourself out of the picture. If you are honest, you and your stuff are the reason you do not honor God, as you should with the tithe. The most difficult thing for ninety percent of us who have not been practicing tithing for any length of time is the ability to forget about us. God, not Melchizedek, blessed Abram (I had always heard it preached that Melchizedek blessed Abram but the blessing came from God who spoke to him personally). Abram is later Abraham once he has a covenant with God. What makes it more interesting is that God released this kind of anointing on a man who is not in covenant with him, "I am your shield, your exceedingly great reward." He is saying, "I am very great. I am all of that. Everything you need is in me."

Listen to the anointing that God releases to Abram who is not in covenant with God but honors the Lord with tithe. The first anointing is that he is protected. Most of us think that all the anointing does is give you ability. You need more than ability. If your whole life was a fight and you never had a time of rest, you would be dead right now. Thank God for the anointing that allow for rest. If you are going to honor the Lord as he is to be honored by the tithe, then you have to forget about yourself. It is a principle that is absolutely, positively, necessary. There is one thing that the enemy will always get your mind on in order to get you to be unfaithful to God, which is focusing on yourself. In the New Testament, the rich young ruler asks, "What is it that I lack?" When he is asked to do something with everything that he possesses, he loses his cool. God says, "I am your great reward."

The scripture says that in a vision the word of the Lord came to Abram. That word is a davar in Hebrew, and it means "the commandment" and/or "a report." The difference between davar and logos is that logos is the manifested thought of God, while davar is the result of that which is manifested. If I have the logos, I have what God is thinking because of what God says. Davar is what happens when he speaks. When he says to Abram, "I am your shield," God was reporting, or commanding, a shield. God was commanding the shield.

What is interesting is that Abram needed a shield for that time. He had just come out of battle and taken spoils. Anytime you go to war and run your enemy to great lengths, there is always the return battle. Read the history, they always come back. The enemy returns for one reason, they return because the fight and your pursuit to conquer took great energy. The men should be tired, and they assume your guard is down. God commanded a shield because Abram had just come out of battle.

God established in Abram's life an anointing for things he does not see and is not prepared for. The first pattern of tithe is that there is not only anointing from the Lord to become one's shield, but God commands something to exist in your life that you are not prepared for. The anointing in your life causes you to withstand the things you are not prepared for, things you aren't thinking of or counting on that you cannot see. Anybody who has been caught by surprise enough knows it is important to have an anointing that protects from those events for which no preparation has been made.

If you think about it, it is always the things you are not prepared for that keep you from being faithful with the tithe. It's that or just blatant disobedience. So, God gives you the kind of anointing that prevents a cycle in your life for the things you are not prepared for. It is a blessing to be able to confess, "I have an anointing to withstand the things I am not prepared for."

I am a tither, a faithful tither. You know what kind of anointing I have in my life? I have the kind of anointing that covers my back. Confess that, you can't make that confession if you are not a tither or not a consistent tither. Consistency is important because if you are not consistent, something could happen the very time that the shield is not up. Don't think that the things you are not prepared for only have to do with money. Most of you probably deal with money issues, but there are a whole lot of things in your life that you need the protection of God for.

God is not just rebuking the devourer and keeping away the locusts on your finances, but also there is an anointing for my children and the generations after me. I am covered and shielded from things I cannot see and that by itself is worth tithing. It is worth a dime on a dollar.

Leviticus 27:30 reads, ***"All of the tither of the land, whether of the seed of the land, or the fruit of the tree, is the Lord's."*** When I tithe, I am acknowledging that everything is God's. If I don't tithe, I am acknowledging that God is not the owner of everything and that I should not look for God to be in control of everything. I should not hold him accountable because he is not in charge of it. That's like going to a company and wanting the janitor to pay you because you fell. The janitor cannot pay for anything; he just forgot to mop the water. Somebody on the top floor has to pay or meet you in court. The janitor does not own the company.

I acknowledge that God is the owner of everything; the sea of the land, the fruit of the tree, or whatever is holy to the Lord. The word *holy* means, "set apart" and "unapproachable." Everything on the earth is the Lord's, and it obviously is not set apart or unapproachable to God; but for anybody else it is set apart and unapproachable. You cannot touch it. Everything on the earth is the Lord's and you cannot approach it. God is not playing; he is serious about the grass, trees, seed, fruit, and air. God is so serious about proper stewardship that he is angry when you don't wash your car.

God is serious about everything in the earth because everything in the earth is holy to him. Adam and Eve were kicked out of the garden for eating from the unapproachable fruit. We should not have access to breathing; we should be dead, but think of the magnitude of his grace in allowing us to use his things for provision. It's a low-down man who will eat your bread and on the way out take all of the crystal settings and food out of the refrigerator when you think something is left to eat later. We should not have access to air, trees, and the things of the earth because they are holy to the Lord, but in his grace he allow us to use the air, even when we are not holy.

God does not require anything of you to breathe. We need the sun to survive, and we have access to that, free of charge. Out of all that is holy and free, all he asks is for one dime out of a dollar. There would be a line from Galveston to San Antonio if there was somebody saying, "The word for ten cents." You would camp out three days early for the sale.

According to Leviticus 27:30-33 it says, **"Concerning the tithe of the herd or the flock and everything that passes under the rod, the tenth one shall be holy unto the Lord…he shall not inquire whether it is good or bad nor shall he exchange it. If he exchanges it at all then both it and the one exchanged for it shall be holy. It shall not be redeemed."** In other words, if I was the tenth one and I had a blemish or two on me and you decided that you didn't want to give God the one with the little blemish and decided to give another to God instead, the other must come to God, in addition. The scriptures say, "These are the commandments which the Lord commanded Moses for the children of Israel on Mt. Sinai." Tithe has changed; the first pattern we saw in Genesis came from the heart saying, "Forget about me, I just love God like that". With every pattern there is an anointing and one pattern was in the book of Genesis.

Deuteronomy 12:1-9 reads, **"These are the statutes and judgments, which you shall be careful to observe in the land which the Lord God of your fathers is giving you to possess, all the days that you live on the earth. You shall utterly destroy all the places where the nations, which you shall dispossess, served their gods on the high mountains and on the hills and under every green tree. And you shall destroy their altars, break their sacred pillars, and burn their wooden images with fires; you shall cut down the carved images of their gods and destroy their games from that place. You shall not worship the Lord your God with such things. (Don't borrow anything from anywhere and worship the Lord with it)But you shall seek the place where the Lord your God chooses out of all your tribes, to put His name for His dwelling place; and there you shall go. There you shall take your burnt offerings, your sacrifices, your tithes, the heave offerings of your hand, your vowed offerings, your freewill offerings, and the firstborn of your herds and flocks and there you shall eat before the Lord your God, and you shall rejoice in all to which you have put your hand, you and** *your households in which the Lord your god has blessed you. You shall not at all do as we are doing here today…every man doing whatever is right in his own eyes…for as yet you have not come to the rest and the inheritance which the Lord your God is giving you."*

In the midst of the offerings that God asks for, God says, *"Bring the tithe to the place that I have chosen."* He asks us to bring it and bring it consistently. Now if we look at it dispensationally then it would mean we were in rest and would not need to bring the tithe. God says, *"Bring the tithe to the place I have chosen, be consistent in bringing it because you have not entered into the place of your rest."* In other words, you have not received everything God has promised you. The fourth anointing on bringing the tithe and being consistent with it is that it keeps you positioned to receive the rest of what God is going to bring to you.

You don't have an opportunity to stop bringing the tithe because you don't have everything yet. You can't afford not to tithe because everything that is coming to you has not made it to you yet. You have to keep the way open for the rest of the things that God is bringing to you.

You have to keep the way open for blessings for your children, fighting for you in warfare and keeping you covered. My inheritance is connected to my tithe. If you have all of your inheritance, you are about to be beamed up out of here. When you come to the place that God has set, you are out of here.

If I am not yet the receiver of my full inheritance in God, then I need to understand that the anointing of the tithe keeps me out of the hands of want so I will be all sufficient. If not, I am never sufficient in anything. Some of you are gloomy and messed up in the mind because you don't always have everything you need. Some of you are messed up because pride has you.

Now, for fifteen years I have said, "Favor is better than money." Sometimes it means that God has other resources. You may not want to ask anybody for anything, but you do not know how God has prepared the hearts of those you are to approach. You need to hear from God by night in a vision.

Tithing keeps me open for the rest of the things that God wants to release in my life. You are not in a position to tie anything up. In fact, you need something to break like a dam under pressure. Things get tied up because you want to operate in disobedience. There is a purpose in God's church for the tithe. It provides for the Levite and provides ministry for the widow, the fatherless, and the orphans. As much as there is a purpose on it, there is an anointing that rests on it.

The lesson continues in Deuteronomy 12:10-14, *"But when you cross over the Jordan and dwell in the land which the Lord your God is giving you to inherit, and He gives you rest from your enemies round about, so that you dwell in safety, (remember Abram and the shield was his promise – the shield would be a rest) then there will be the place where the Lord your God chooses to make His name abide. There you shall bring all that I command you: your burnt offerings, your sacrifices, your tithes, the heave offerings of your hand, and all your choice offerings which you vow to the Lord. And you shall rejoice before the Lord your God, you and your sons and your daughters, your male and female servants, and the Levite who is within your gates, since he has no portion nor inheritance with you. Take heed to yourself that you do not offer your burnt offerings in every place that you see; but in the place which the Lord chooses."*

Then Deuteronomy 12:17-19 tells us, *"You may not eat within your gates the tithe of your grain or your new wine or your oil, of the firstborn of your herd or your flock, of any of your offerings which you bow of your freewill offerings, or the heave offering of your hand, but you must eat them before the Lord your god in the place which the Lord your God chooses…you shall rejoice before the Lord your God…Take heed to yourself that you do not forsake the Levite as long as you live in your land."* You have to take care of the Levites. It is a command of God to take care of the Levites. That is not the pastor, but the workers of the ministry. The people who work in the ministry suffer enough working for you; they should not have to suffer in their living.

God said, "You cannot eat the tithe in any place." You shall not eat your tithe except you eat it before the Lord in the place he has chosen: you shall not consume your tithe. The bible says that everything that is in the earth belongs to the Lord and is called holy.

A wave offering is waved before God. God would thereby accept it. Rams, lambs, and other animals were burned. On the offerings accepted by God, they must be consumed; they may be eaten or fire may consume them, but they cannot be consumed outside of the order of God.

If the order of God is to bring the tithe to take care of the Levite as long as you are in the land, it means it should not be consumed anywhere else. It should not pay my car note or pay my rent; it may have helped you once or twice. God says, "If you hold on to it and do something else with it, the tithe must be still brought with a fifth part brought with it." Your tithe is not to be consumed anywhere else. "Well, God understands," one might say. Yes, but God also has an order that says it should not be consumed outside of the order of God. If you consume it elsewhere, you are in violation. If the offering is to be burned, imagine eating something on fire. The idea is that, that which you consume, consumes you. If you ever fall into a place where you stop honoring the order of the Lord, it is very difficult to come back. You become consumed with what you consume, and it is very difficult to bring it back to the Lord because you have conditioned yourself to consume it. You are taking down your shield, cursing your children and missing the protection of it. Your tithe returns to you in relationships, your career, and in every area of your life.

As tight as money may get, can you afford the lack of anointing? I want my passage to stay open. The openings of the windows are an obvious anointing. Some of us never pay attention to open windows. The anointing that we discover is coming out of the windows like water. The Holy Spirit, which is a sign of the anointing, is the shield, the passage, and the blessing of the generations. All are being poured out of the windows, not just one thing is covered, God is blessing in a multiplicity of anointing through the tithe. When you start talking about the things I am not prepared for, those things alone are enough for me to say, "Here, take it and more."

Chapter 4

THE BIBLICAL EXPECTATION:

Then the Lord spoke to Moses, saying, "Speak thus to the Levites, and say to them: "When you take from the children of Israel the tithes which I have given you from them as your inheritance, then you shall offer up a heave offering of it to the Lord, a tenth of the tithe. And your heave offering shall be reckoned to you as though it were the grain of the threshing floor and as the fullness of the winepress. Thus you shall also offer a heave offering unto the Lord from all your tithes which you receive from the children of Israel, and you shall give the Lord's heave offering from it to Aaron the priest." Numbers 18:25-28

There is an order on the tithe as well as an anointing. If you bring a tenth of the tithe, God considers the tenth of the tithe of the Levites as the grain of the threshing floor. This was the abundance offering that God considered for himself. A threshing floor offering is the Lord's.

God is saying, "I am going to take the tithe that Israel is to bring to the house and give it to the Levites. The tenth of the tithe will be given to the priest, and it will be considered a grain offering, which is his." The Levites are to give a tithe of the tithe to the priest. It will be considered to be the best of the best offerings, which is given to the Lord. A tithe of the tithe is given to the priest. They return it to the house, which is the priest.

Failure for you to give the tithe profanes every other gift you give. Giving the tithe makes everything else you have holy for the tithe is holy. So then, everything else behind the tithe is also called holy because the tithe is holy. I cannot really release to God an offering until I release the tithe.

If the anointing that is on the tithe makes everything else holy then understand what happens to that which is holy. Anything that is holy has to be consumed by fire; that is the only way the Lord can consume t. One of the instructions of the Lord to the children of Israel was to get the holy things out of their house.

Deuteronomy 26:12-13 is where we discover what the rest of the money should be doing. "When you have finished laying aside all of the tithe of your increase in the third year – they year of tithing – and have given it to the Levite, the stranger, the fatherless, and the widow, so that they may eat within your gates and be filled, then you shall say before the Lord your God, I have removed the holy tithe from my house, and also have given them to the Levite, the stranger, the fatherless, and the widow, according to all your commandments which you have commanded me; I have not transgressed your commandments, nor have I forgotten them."

The command is to get the holy thing out of your house. Anyone who is holding onto the holy thing that is to be consumed by fire should expose the rest of his things to be consumed. To hold the tithe is to burn the rest. You need to get the holy thing out of your house.

When you take the holy thing out of your house, you take curses out. If you get the holy thing out of your house, you take curses out of your life that would come if you kept it. Anybody who kept the holy thing in their house had to die: they, their children, and everything of theirs had to be burned.

The second thing that happens when tithing is seen in verses 14-15, *"I have not eaten any of it when in neither mourning, nor have I removed any of it for an unclean use, nor given any of it for the dead. I have obeyed the voice of the Lord my God, and have done according to all that you have commanded me. Look down from your holy habitation, from heaven, and bless your people Israel and the land which you have given us, just as you swore to our fathers," a land flowing with milk and honey."* The tithe activates the promises of God in your life. Tithing is like a propeller, a tail wind that pushes you toward the things God has promised.

Then verses 16-17 read, *"This day the Lord your God commands you to observe these statutes and judgments; therefore you shall be careful to observe them with all of your heart and with all your soul."* God is saying don't play with this. Today you have proclaimed that the Lord is your God, that you will walk in his ways to keep his commandments and his judgments, and that you will obey his voice. Also, today the Lord has proclaimed you to be special. If you claim that the Lord is God in your life, you are going to obey his voice; if you proclaim that you are going to be honorable before God, then today God proclaims you are special. The day you honor God with your tithe is the day he proclaims you special. The word is *segullah*, which means *"possessions"* and/or *"jewel."* When you look at the word special, you are not just talking about jewels or possessions, but also the anointing that comes from releasing the tithe and proclaiming God to be your God. Proclaiming to obey his voice releases God to hold you like property.

Property is important to God because property suggests dominion. If you operate within the rule of dominion, God now has you as his property. You are the possession of God, and he is ruling not just in your life, but to protect you and everything else in your life. Tithing then becomes insurance on everything you possess. God says, "When you become special, I claim you, and when I claim you, I claim everything that you have. Just as I am going to protect you, I have to protect everything that you have."

Verse 19 indicates something else about the tithe: *"And that He will set you high above all nations which he has made, in praise, in name, and in honor and that you may be a holy people to the Lord your God just as He has spoken."* When I release the tithe, I release an anointing on my life; the purpose of God becomes fulfilled in me. I release the anointing for purpose in my life.

If you have no sense of destiny, releasing the anointing may neither excite nor bother you. If you can taste the purpose of God in your life or taste God moving in your life and if you know now like you never knew before that God was visiting you, then this text says by being faithful in the tithe, you release the anointing of God so that whatever he says about you has to come to pass.

There is an anointing on the tithe. When you look at the word special in verse 18, it is the same: one means *"possession"* and the other means *"jewel"* (see Malachi 3:17). Remember he says the day that you proclaim you are going to obey him is the day he is going to proclaim you are special to him. The anointing to the tithe releases the anointed to discern. It is amazing there is an anointing on tithe that releases the anointed to discern. It is amazing that I can dull spiritual discernment because I will not honor the Lord with the tithe. That's why things can sneak up on you without benefit of discernment through your spiritual senses. When you tithe, whatever has been dulling your spiritual senses gets moved.

Most believers do not realize they have dulled spiritual senses; everything is status quo and the apostolic anointing means nothing. An apostolic anointing does the following: it solidifies and makes sure that you are a jewel. It makes the quality of life better for people: you become a better husband, wife, money manager, or whatever you are going to become. You will be a better one of those. God releases an apostolic anointing to you that makes your life better. Things do not just get better, you get better. There's an anointing on tithing, and nothing else carries that same anointing.

Deuteronomy 14:22 tells us, *"You shall truly tithe all the increase of your grain."* In Deuteronomy, we read every third was the year of tithing. Every three years, each person was expected to bring to the Lord an offering that was a tithe, an extra tithe. It was a holy year, a divine year. It was a year set apart and a year of anointing. Anybody who has experienced this understands that if you want to make changes in your life, plan to do so every third year, in the year of anointing, because it releases debt. God reminds us in Deuteronomy 14:27-28: *"You shall not forsake the Levite…At the end of every third year you shall bring out the tithe of your produce of that year and store it up within your gates. The Levite, because he has no portion or inheritance…may…be satisfied, that the Lord your God may bless you in all the work of your hand which you do."*

Operating in the third year, the tithe not only brings the surplus to the house of God, it releases anointing on the house for becoming debt free. If the house of God has a surplus from the third-year tithe and the house is able to operate debt free, then that which is in the house flows to those who are within the house.

God has an anointing on tithe and a principle for it to operate and you must do it in the way that he says it has to be done. If the house rests debt free, then the people of the house rest debt free. You cannot speak debt free into the lives of people if you are not debt free. How do you expect the church to transfer something to you that it does not possess?

The third-year tithe as surplus releases vision. The anointing on tithe releases vision. Why? If it operates in the third year and brings about a surplus and releases debt, then there is no need to release ministry that has to be financed because everything needed is already there. If you are not tithing, you are holding up vision, and you are stifling the vision of the man of God. If he cannot build what God has already spoken, then he cannot see what God has further. You stop the vision when you do not tithe, yet the tithe takes care of the Levites of the house. Let vision go; release it.

II Chronicles 31:2-10, *"And Hezekiah appointed the divisions of the priests and the Levites according to their divisions, each man according to his service, the priests and the Levites for burnt offerings and peace offerings, to serve, to give thanks, and to praise in the gates of the camp of the Lord. The king also appointed a portion of his possessions for the burnt offerings; for the morning and evening burnt offerings; the burnt offerings for the Sabbaths, and the New Moons and the set feasts, as it is written in the Law of the Lord. Moreover he commanded the people who dwelt in Jerusalem to contribute support for the priests and the Levites, that they might devote themselves to the Law of the Lord. As soon as the commandment as circulated, the children of Israel brought in abundance the firstfruits of grain and wine, oil and honey, and all of the produce of the field; and they brought in abundantly the tithe of everything. And the children of Israel and Judah, who dwelt in the cities of Judah, brought the tithe of oxen and sheep; also the tithe of holy things which were consecrated to the Lord their God they laid in heaps. In the third month they began laying them in heaps, and they finished in the seventh month. And when Hezekiah and the leaders came and saw the heaps, they blessed the Lord and his people Israel. Then Hezekiah questioned the priests and Levites concerning the heaps. And Azariah the chief priest, from the house of Zadok, answered him and said, Since the people began to bring the offerings into the house of the Lord, we have had enough to eat and have plenty left, for the Lord has blessed his people; and what is left is this great abundance."*

Verse 18 reads, *"All who were written in the genealogy – their little ones and their wives, their sons and daughters, the whole company of them – for in their faithfulness they sanctified themselves in holiness."*

One of the anointings on the tithe is that you sanctify yourself in holiness; you release the anointing on the tithe to trickle down from family to family, all the verses I skipped over say this. The anointing you clap your hands for may not be coming because your neighbor is not tithing. Tell your neighbor to get his hand out of your pocket. There are some things that should be flowing to you that cannot because your neighbor is not sanctified to holiness where nothing can hurt you, where God can help you, and where you are in a fruitful place. You have no idea what kind of anointing you keep out of your life.

This is no longer an individual anointing. Now there is a corporate anointing released if the people of the house will bless the house. Now, there is obedience for others' blessings, homes, and children. Your brothers and sisters are your keeper.

II Chronicles chapter 32:1-8 indicates there is not only a corporate anointing. The same anointing on your life makes officials recognize you. Certain pastors have a favor with certain city officials because there is somewhere a group of people who releases that type of anointing on the man of God. This causes the man of God to be able to get your child out of jail, just by making a phone call. He has the kind of anointing that has influence and favor with city officials.

There is an anointing on tithe that makes quality of life better for every man who will honor God with a dime on every dollar. You cannot bless your children's legacy for ten cents, have favor with city officials, and have a healing anointing by yourself, but with God you will have this anointing.

II Chronicles 31:5 indicates several things, when you are faithful in tithing, there is an anointing that you release on your life that sanctifies you in holiness. Everything you have remaining in your hands after you have given to the Lord is holy, also. Anything sanctified is spiritually sanctified by the anointing. The reason the remaining ninety percent (90%) gets lost or messed up is that you do not mix it with the right morality. I don't care how much you do, according to what is written, where you are not living right is a major gate for spiritual darkness, rulers of darkness, witchcraft, and other sources of darkness to gain entrance into your life.

The greatest entrance for darkness to perform any activity in your life is not through your drink, but is through not living right. One of the things we learn is we sanctify ourselves in holiness through the tithe. In II Chronicles chapter 32:1-8 there is the indication that vision is released and recognition comes from government officials. You release the man of God into favor for things he would never have been able to buy.

There is no sense in marveling that T.D. Jakes is given hundreds of acres of land through former Texas Governor George Bush, the tithe releases power to do work that is of God that causes others to take note. Men will pass by and call you a delightsome land. What you could have never paid for God will give you.

When we are faithful with the tithe, we cause everyone around us to prosper. Is your hand in your neighbor's pocket? Because you are connected, your neighbor can interfere with your progress toward prosperity. I am not prospering because my neighbor is bringing a curse to the house, you may think. It is the easiest thing to change churches, going where things look prosperous, but you can bring curses to them. Tithe in your own house, take your hand out of your neighbor's pocket, and make your own house and church prosper. It is not solely between your neighbor and God, but it involves your finances, too.

If you are not tithing, you are a coward. You are operating in fear and afraid of what you cannot see, but you serve a God you cannot see. Tithing is supposed to make me, my legacy, and my children blessed. Everything around me is to be blessed. Verses 20 and 21 indicate that when people are tithing, every good work that is envisioned by the man of God goes forth. Then, it is nothing for the man of God to cause what you are trying to do to go forth.

Recently, we took an offering according to the call of God and paid a young lady's bills. I believe her debt was wiped out, and I believe some of that anointing was for everybody around her. You need to speak to your fellow members if they are not tithing and say, "We need to talk; we will not fight, but we need to talk."

Nehemiah 13:4-12 reads, *"Now before this, Eliashib the priest, having authority over the storerooms of the house of our God, was allied with Tobiah. And he had prepared for him a large room, where previously they had stored the grain offerings, the frankincense, the articles, the tithes of grain, the new wind and oil, which were commanded to be given to the Levites and singers and gatekeepers, and the offerings for the priests, but during all this I was not in Jerusalem, for in the thirty-second year of Artaxerxes king of Babylon I had returned to the king. Then after certain days I obtained leave from the king, and I came to Jerusalem and discovered the evil that Eliashib had done for Tobiah, in preparing a room for him n the courts of the house of God. And it grieved me bitterly; therefore I threw all the household goods of Tobiah out of the room. Then I commanded them to cleanse the rooms' and I brought back into them the artifles of the house of God, with the grain offering and the frankincense. I also realized that the portions for the Levites had not been given them; for each of the Levites and the singers who did the work had gone back to his field. So I contended with the rulers, and said, "Why is the house of God forsaken?" And I gathered them together and set them in their place. Then all of Judah brought the tithe of the grain and the new wine and the oil to the storehouse."*

One of the reasons why Tobias brought the goods into the house of God is because the people would not follow the rules: the room was empty. Now, Elisha was not supposed to be allied with Tobias. When you are unfaithful with the tithe, it forces you to have to make unholy alliances. You connect yourself to things that God has not commanded, like second jobs and sugar daddies and mamas. It forces you to make too many unholy alliances, request loans, and sell yourself to places God has not called you to sell out to. When you are not faithful with the tithe, you are going to replace it with something. You will have to commit to something unholy, something that God did not ordain. You may say, "I am trying to make it. Got to do what I can to get by, trying to keep some bread in the box, food in the house, clothes on my back, and the lights on." And the truth of the matter is that you are catching hell trying to do that. You cannot do it. So, when you wake up and realize that if not tithing is not making it any easier, perhaps you need to find God's way of doing things.

Tobias suggests the freedom of the priest in this passage, Nehemiah 13:4-12. The only reason Nehemiah said he had to come back was that the house was out of order. If the priest can only tend to the house and work in the house, then no vision for anything greater will ever be given and all you will have is a house. If you want more to happen, you have to free your priest up to do it.

Don't force your church into unholy alliances. Favor says the world is supposed to give to me; they have got to come, **"Good measure, shaken together."** Don't force your church to depend on them. Be faithful and you will sanctify yourself.

The anointing of the tithe can be limited if morally there is no accountability. Matthew 23:20-26 reads, **"Therefore, he who swears by the altar, swears by it and by all things on it. He who swears by the temple swears by it and by all things on it. He, who swears by the temple, swears by Him who dwells in it. And he, who swears by heaven, swears by the throne of God and by Him who sits on it. Woe to you, scribes and Pharisees, hypocrites! For you pay tithe of mint and anise and cumin, and have neglected the weightier matters of the law: justice and mercy and faith. These you ought to have done, without leaving the others undone. Blind guides, who strain out a gnat and swallow a came! Woe to you, scribes and Pharisees hypocrites! For you cleanse the outside of the cup and dish, but inside they are full of extortion and self-indulgence. Blind Pharisee, first cleanse the inside of the cup and dish, that the outside of them may be clean also."**

I can limit the anointing that comes with the tithe because morally there is no accountability. God does not just want a rich, prosperous people, he wants a holy people. One thing in the church that seems to be the problem of many is that we do not want to be told how to live. We want to be prosperous and know about relationships. We are in a different day when holy men must be holy and righteous people must be righteous.

I can limit the anointing because I just will not live right. I can maximize the anointing with virtue and Godliness. If I can practice the principles of God and have anointing too then hell does not like that. If you are oozing with favor, then you should not be depending on everybody for everything, and you cannot buy yourself a loaf of bread. It is the will of God that what comes out of you is what God puts in and on you such that your life mirrors the promises of God. This will not happen one day, it will happen today." Today I have and today I am, you will maximize the anointing that God has on your life if you learn how to be faithful with the tithe.

Nehemiah 10:37 and 39 tell us, **"To bring the firstfruits of our dough, our offerings, the fruit from all kinds of trees, the new wine and oil, to the priests, to the storerooms of the house of our God; and to bring the tithes of our land to the Levites, for the Levites should receive the tithes in all our farming communities…for the children of Israel and the children of Levi shall bring the offering of the grain, of the new wine and the oil, to the storerooms where the articles of the sanctuary are, where the priests who minister and the gatekeepers and the singers are; and we will not neglect the house of our God."**

Again, he is talking about bringing the tithe to the storehouse. Leviticus 37:31 indicates Hezekiah the priest found that people brought the tithe so faithfully that it was in heaps, and they sanctified themselves. He literally had to build rooms to hold the tithe.

We want the kind of anointing that God says comes from tithing: *"The windows of heaven will be open that there will not be room enough to receive it."* Is God a bad steward? Will he just waste what you cannot hold? In Leviticus it says Hezekiah prepared rooms. We want God to give us things that we don't have room enough to receive. It is coming because we have rooms prepared to receive.

You don't have any money to invest, but that does not stop you from talking to an investor. If you want God to give you the kind of blessings and you don't have room enough to receive, you have to prepare rooms. He did not say don't prepare rooms. You took it that God is going to pour things out, not that you need to get ready. Don't miss what he is telling you, this is an Old Testament pattern. If God is going to give us so much that we do not have room enough to receive, and then prepare the room. Talk to a financial planner, even if you only have a nickel or a dime. You need to scope things out.

You cannot talk to financial advisors without the inspiration to do what they are talking about. If you want a not-room-enough blessing, you have got to prepare rooms. That is talking to investors, planners and people with those skills to prepare for the thing God is going to release to you. Don't get mad at people who are prospering.

Haggai 1:3-9 reads, *"Then the word of the lord came by Haggai the prophet, saying, Is it time for you yourselves to dwell in your paneled houses, and this temple to lie in ruins?" Now, therefore, thus says the Lord of hosts: Consider your ways! You have sown much and bring in little; you eat, but do not have enough; you drink, but you are not filled with drink. You clothe yourselves, but no one is warm; and he who earns wages earns wages to put into a bag with holes. Thus says the Lord of hosts: Consider your ways! Go up to the mountains and bring wood and build the temple, that I may take pleasure in it and be glorified, says the Lord. You look for much, but indeed it came too little; and when you brought home, I blew it away. Why, says the Lord of hosts? Because of my house that is in ruins, while everyone of you runs to his own house."*

God called for a drought on all the labor of your hands. Now, I didn't make that up. If you are working and don't have enough, you are either living beyond your means or you have holes in your bag. God blew on it. You are bringing in a whole lot, but still you have nothing. Nehemiah and Haggai tell us if we want to release the curses, we must tithe. Consider your ways, I want you to be faithful with the tithe so none of us will be cursed because it is contagious. Because you are my sister and brother, I am compelled sometimes to help you when you are in trouble. The only thing I am doing is taking what I have that is good and putting it in your hands that are cursed. How am I suppose to bless you and you are cursed? If you do what you are supposed to, you will not need mine.

There is a fine line and we are confused. If the church does not help you, then you think the church is wrong, but you are the reason why you are in trouble, tithe and God will sew up the holes and stop blowing on your finances.

Deuteronomy 28:36-39 promises us, *"The Lord will bring you and the king whom you set over you to a nation…you shall become astonishment, a proverb, and a byword among all nations where the Lord will drive you...for the locust shall consume (and) you shall plant vineyards and tend them (but) the worms shall eat them."*

You ask yourself why is it everybody else around you is being blessed and you go lower and lower. You cannot disobey God and expect to have anointing. The most tragic thing as a believer is to conjure in your head that the only people God will bless are believers. God says, **"It rains on the just and the unjust,"** and people who believe in the principles prosper. But here you are in a relationship with God and not prospering because you will not practice the principles that has laid out you. You cannot even anoint yourself; you could not find an anointing to come out of the life you have made for yourself, even if you tried.

Chapter 5

THE DIVINE COVENANT

"And Jacob went out from Beersheba, and went toward Haran. And he lighted upon a certain place, and tarried there all night, because the sun was set; and he took of the stones of that place, and put them for his pillows, and lay down in that place to sleep. And he dreamed, and behold a ladder set upon the earth, and the top of it reached to heaven: and behold the angels of God ascending and descending on it. And, behold, the Lord stood above it, and said, I am the Lord God of Abraham thy father, and the God of Isaac: the land whereon thou liest, to thee will I give it, and to thy seed." Genesis 28:10-13

Tithe connects you in covenant with God. We tap into things through the link of the tithe that preserves everything that we possess. If the tithe is holy and belongs to the Lord and is devoted to the Lord, it is accursed, which means it is set apart to the Lord, to be received of the Lord by burning. It is a devoted, holy thing unto the Lord. There is a covering for everything we possess by honoring God in the tithe.

Genesis 28:10-13 says, *"Now Jacob went out from Beersheba and went toward Haran. So he came to a certain place and stayed there all night, because the sun had set. And he took one of the stones of that place and put it at his head, and he lay down in that place to sleep. Then he dreamed, and behold, a ladder was set up on the earth, and its top reached to heaven; and there the angels of God were ascending and descending on it. And behold, the Lord stood above it and said: I am the Lord God of Abraham your father and the God of Isaac; and the land on which you lie I will give you and your descendents."*

In verses 20-22, the story continues, *"Then Jacob made a vow, saying, "If God will be with me, and keep me in this way that I am going, and give me bread to eat and clothing to put on, so that I come back to my father's house in peace, then the Lord shall be my God. And this stone which I have set as a pillar shall be God's house, and of all that You give me I will surely give a tenth to you."*

There is no agreement between Jacob and God prior to the dream to tithe. Abram tithed because he loved the Lord. Jacob does not have that experience. Jacob has a dream; and all of this time he is living under the blessing of Abram. As a result of a personal encounter with God, he no longer decides to rest under the blessing of Abraham. He said, "If God said He was going to do all that, then of everything He gives me, I am going to give a tithe."

31

Everything that God promised Jacob was the promise of God without Jacob doing anything.. The heart of Jacob says to God, "If you dare to bless me, if you dare to keep me, if you dare to be with me, then here is my response to you, God: I will give you a tithe of everything." He tapped into the promises of God by honoring the tithe because God was with him, not because of the law. Many of you may want to deny the anointing of God, but you cannot deny that he has been with you. If you know he has been with you and has been keeping you, then your response should be, "If you are going to be with me, I am going to give you a tenth of everything you give me."

How do you give a tenth of God being with you back? We owe him to worship him and to be in his presence. If he is with us twenty-four/seven, we owe him twenty-four/seven. I owe him at least two and a half days of my week. This is for Christ's people everywhere. "It is tight; Lord," you say, but he says "Prove me."

In Joshua 6:12,17, and 18,we read, *"And Joshua rose early in the morning, and the priests took up the ark of the Lord...(Joshua said,) Now the city shall be doomed by the Lord to destruction, it and all who are in it. Only Rahab the harlot shall live, she and all who are with her in the house, she hid the messengers that we sent. And you, by all means abstain from the accursed things, lest you become accursed when you take of the accursed things, and make the camp of Israel a curse, and trouble it."*

Rahab the harlot is saved because she hid the spies, the messengers of God, who also honored the Lord with the tithe. She was saved fooling with folk who tithe. God saved a harlot who found herself dealing with people who dedicated the tithe to the Lord. Joshua 7 indicates that when the children of Israel went to battle against a small group, they should have won with ease, but had no anointing to take. In verse 11, we learn, "Israel has sinned and they have also transgressed My covenant...For they have even taken some of the accursed things, and have both stolen and deceived; and they have also put it among their own stuff."

God saves a harlot because she covers those who tithe and then kills his own people because they don't, because they stole, and because they deceived: "Neither will I be with you anymore before you destroy the accursed that is among you."

Let us say we are sending three people to whip a midget in a war. They don't come back because they die in battle, and we wonder how? When you fail to honor the Lord with the tithe, you forfeit your own anointing to accomplish the tasks before you by God with ease because somebody steals the tithe. He saves a harlot who is not his, but kills his own. Achin buried something in his house, Joshua had to line them up, one by one, family by family, and say, "Who did it?" Tithing is a corporate responsibility. This is an anointing that you are preventing yourself from receiving. Things are not working for you. Check the person who is "skinning and grinning" with you , who says they love you, but will send you out to battle to die.

You think we are supposed to make it because we are the church, but God will allow you to die for disobedience. We are perpetrators who say we love God, but will not fear or obey him. All of us would choose Achin over Rahab. You don't want to be associated with a whore, so you will choose Him. You will let a Rahab die, but you will sit right next to somebody who blatantly disrespects the things of God and call them your brother or sister. You need to make sure that they do it for your sake.

Now I understand why Jesus would rather eat with sinners. At least he had an invitation. The disciples asked, "Why are you going to Zacheus's house?" I can hear him thinking, "You didn't invite me to yours." As much as they were in the region of their house, you never hear of Him eating at their houses. He was always at the house of a sinner.

There is an anointing on the tithe, and there is a corporate responsibility and a corporate destiny. Ask your church member, if they care anything about you? They should not neglect their corporate responsibility by sending you out to die.

Deuteronomy 12:5-7 instructs, ***"But you shall seek the place where the Lord your God chooses, out of all your tribes, to put His name for His dwelling place; and there you shall go. There you shall take your burnt offerings, your sacrifices, your tithes, the heave offerings of your hand, your vowed offerings, your freewill offerings, and the firstborn of your herds and flocks. And there you shall eat before the Lord your God, and you shall rejoice in all to which you have put your hand, you and your households, in which the Lord your God has blessed you."***

The tithe is holy and everything you have left is holy. If the whole is holy, then the whole I should be enjoying. Most of us are living with the whole being stolen. You make it, but you don't enjoy it. God will blow on it because you don't care for the corporate body. God says you and your house should enjoy the rest. Something is wrong, either the management is off or you are living foolishly or somewhere there is an accursed one attached to you, and it may not be the family member who is not saved. Remember Rahab? You cannot go and say, "It is my husband who does not go to church." He might be Rahab; it could be the folk you are connected to corporately. We have been taught in the church to be responsible for our house, and we have not been taught to be responsible for each other in the church.

All of your house may not gather here and in the tithe there is a corporate anointing. Verse 11 reminds you to make "all your choice offerings which you vow to the Lord." There is such an anointing in the tithe that the tithe allows not only you to enjoy it, but also everybody who is connected to you. Corporate anointing either works against or for you. You make up your mind how it is going to work.

Verse 17-19 says, ***"You may not eat within your gates the tithe of your grain or your new wine or your oil, of the firstborn of your herd or your flock, of any of your offerings which you vow; of your freewill offerings, or of the heave offerings of your hand. But you must eat them before the Lord your God in the place which the Lord your God chooses, you and your son and your daughter, your male servant and your female servant, and the Levite who is within your gates; and you shall rejoice before the Lord your God in all to which you put your hands. Take heed to yourself that you do not forsake the Levite as long as you live in your land."***

Take heed you do not forsake the Levite. God is saying to be careful not to consume your tithe. There is a major difference between consuming your tithe where God has not instructed and consuming it where God has instructed. Either way it will be consumed. The anointing is only released when you consume it in front of God. The tithe only receives the anointing that is on it when I bring it to the Lord, not to someone else.

Here is the pattern for tithing. You consume it in too many places. The tithe does not release the anointing for vacation: "Well, pastor I enjoyed myself." The anointing that comes with the tithe is only released when it is consumed before the Lord. If you want to make this work for you, follow the pattern that is right.

It is tight, but does using the tithe help? You used the tithe and the situation did not change because you have to keep using it. God says, "Prove me." I am able to accomplish, as a pastor, whatever I purpose and that is sometimes pretty deep. Whatever god purposes for my life; in God's time shall be accomplished in me. I have been tithing since I was twelve years old, and I am thirty-three at this time. For twenty-one years anything I said I was going to do, I did it. I did not come from a family that would afford for me to do that . I am the baby of my family, and my mother, sisters, and brothers look to me. My sister is able to confess that she has not always been faithful to the tithe; I have always been faithful to the tithe. If you compare where I stand and where my sister stands, they are not the same.

It could be any number of things. We went to the same high school, she received degrees, and she works in major places; could it be the number of years she was not faithful in the tithe? I have always been faithful, everything in our upbringing is the same, she was a pastor too. We have walked the same path.

God says that if you are faithful with the tithe, it sanctifies you, it sets you apart. For twenty-one years I have been faithful, and everything I say I want to do I can and I will. Confirm with me the following: I will accomplish everything I purpose and everything that God has purposed shall be accomplished in my life. I have made up my mind that the tithe is holy and all I possess I shall enjoy; all I confess I shall enjoy. I shall enjoy my marriage, family, wife, children, workplace, my anointing, and my relationship with God. There is nothing in my life I shall not enjoy because I am releasing the anointing of the tithe on my life. I will not steal from God; I will give the accursed thing to God that I may not be a curse. This is what I am releasing in my life today: the ability, anointing, power, strength, persuasion, influence, and the faith to all things God has desired in me. I will not go lacking, I will not miss or fail, I am becoming perfect in all God's ways to do everything God has purposed in my life. I will be a successful, accomplished, favored child of God. I will be an anointed vessel who possesses the world, the heavens and the earth, all that I have is holy. I declare in the name of Jesus, no locust or evil being shall come into my house to destroy anything that I possess. It is mine given to me by God. I shall not lose it, I cannot waste it, and others cannot destroy it. The rest of my life, I am anointed, and the anointing is not only with me, but in me. I will go and be an anointing in someone else's life to achieve corporate destiny and help someone walk through fire and neither be burned or drowned.

There are no mishaps, there are no mistakes, and things do not just haphazardly happen in my life. I am anointed. Believe it, confess it, Amen.

Chapter 6

GOD'S PLAN FOR THE TITHE AND OFFERING

And verily they that are of the sons of Levi, who receive the office of the priesthood, have a commandment to take tithes of the people according to the law, that is, of their brethren, though they come out of the loins of Abraham:

But he whose descent is not counted from them received tithes of Abraham, and blessed him that had the promises.

And without all contradiction the less is blessed of the better. And here men that die receive tithes; but there he receiveth them, of whom it is witnessed that he liveth. Hebrews 7:5-8

In times now, we are living not really knowing or understanding who we really are or the power we have. God is allowing us to experience daily all that he has created us to be. Everything that God is going to give or do through you has not already been done. You have to wait until he proceeds. Either you are not ready or the people he is going to send you too are not ready for you. In any case, both parties have to go through the experiences they must go through in order to build character. There are promises that have been made to you that will not come to pass until character has been established. Have you submitted fully to really learning what God is trying to teach you? Have you ever stopped to think, it is never the devil that stands between you and the promise; but it is usually your character.

It is dangerous when character is standing between you and the promise, and you don't even know it. You are frustrated because you have some sense of what should be happening. You know in the spirit even while you are waiting for it to materialize. Frustration is the manifestation of knowing that reality is actually not what should be. Let frustration push you to character, which is what results when you go through something. You don't develop character from a life that is made up of a cake walk. Character comes from trials. You have got to go through something.

God will let you get frustrated and tired and will let you go through trials and tribulation just so he can build character in you. As noted in Romans 5:4, your hope is your character.

People who are struggling say that it is hard even with the lesson on tithing. I am trying to follow the lead of God because it is so much. For people who are struggling right now saying, "It is hard; it is tight." We can refer to Romans 5:3-5, where it is written, **"And not** *only that, but we also glory in tribulations, knowing that tribulation produces perseverance; and perseverance, character; and character, hope. Now hope does not disappoint, because the love of God has been poured out in our hearts by the Holy Spirit who was given to us."* If you have been cursing troubles and cursing tribulation, understand that tribulation produces endurance and character. The more character is produced in you, the more hope is produced. Hope is the stuff you have been praying for and waiting on. The scripture says, "Hope does not disappoint."

You do not get frustrated for nothing, and you do not go through trial for nothing. God is trying to produce in you the ability to endure. He is trying to produce in you some stick-to-itiveness – how to stay in there until he produces some character. It produces hope, and you get closer to the promise when you go through the trouble. Ask God for grace to go through the process.

I don't lift heavy stuff everyday by myself. I was standing outside with my wife one day, and the wheel of the trailer that held our boat came off, I was doing everything I could when I realized I could not do it myself; finally, I took a drink of water and asked God, "Give me grace to lift this," and I asked my wife to slip a board under it. After the prayer, I was able to lift the twenty-five hundred pounds from the ground up. When I did that, I did not say, "Look at that, girl, I am a he-man", I said, "Look at God, He gave me grace."

When you are going through trials and tribulations, learning to endure, ask him for grace to go through it. You will discover that there is ability in you given to you by the Holy Ghost to make it, overcome, and come through. There is a grace given to you by God in the person of the Holy Ghost to bring you out. God is just trying to teach you how to endure to produce character in you.

There are some of you who find it a challenge just to tithe. If you could just persevere and endure it! Then character develops, and the promises of God will come to pass. We want to attempt to answer the challenge of God and expect immediately the promises. The promises come after you have endured. You need to really learn how the tithe works.

You want the great blessings of God. Anointing deals with protecting you and releasing you. It does not do a whole lot in the way of releasing money. A lot of us are looking to the tithe for increase. The tithe is a covenant connector, a covering, protection, release, and favor. It has to have something to cover if it works as a covering.

The tithe is holy and it makes everything you possess holy. We will give the tithe, but we will expect the magnificent blessing. The tithe is what makes everything else work. To give my offering without the connection, protection, and favor is not doing me any good. If I gave the tithe and no offering, the tithe is waiting to protect something, but it has nothing to protect. It is waiting to go to work, but it has nothing to work with. God says, "Bring the tithe and the offering." There is a way the tithe works. The tithe works for your offering so that everything you give in the offering is holy because the tithe is holy. Everything you have in your hand is holy because the tithe is holy.

You want the tithe to protect the rest of your seed or fruit so the locusts cannot devour it (Malachi 3). The tithe works as the door opener. God says it opens windows: "You bring it, and I will open windows." Here is the tithe; I have release it to God, but I have to give it something to work with. Without an offering you have tithe (which is favor) with nothing to do.

My conviction about this was so great that I began to take an offering equal to my tithe. I have been a faithful tither: I had the covenant connector, favor and protection, but what was the tithe protecting? Acts 21:26 *"Then Paul took the men, and the next day, having been purified with them, entered the temple to announce the expiration of the days of purification, at which time an offering should be made for each of them."*

Paul said they were coming to the end of the days of the period of sanctification, and every man was to bring an offering – *prospherah* - which means *prosperous*. What is then in the offering? Prosperity; why do we look for it in the tithe? The tithe has to have something to work with. The tithe opens the door for you to prosper, but you release the *prospherah* through the offering. In Malachi 3, God says, "I will rebuke the devourer." He promised to pour out blessings the same as rain, and we know locusts cannot move when it is wet. God is saying, "I will prevent the locusts from eating up your crops before time." But what releases the action is the offering you send with the tithe. This is for every man who believes, not just the Jews.

The tithe brings covenant, covering, protection, and favor. It brings strength to you and protection from the battles you are not even aware of. If I want the prosperity, the prosperity does not come because of the tithe. The tithe only protects the offering. The tithe covers every seed I have, my every protection. If I want the favor of prosperity, I have to give an offering. The offering is unacceptable without the tithe.

Israel brought offerings, but God was angry because they did not bring the tithe. They were cut off because the Levites were left out. The offering is unacceptable without the tithe. You can look at it as the law or God bringing favor on you. After the tithe, the offering is released to work. If we want to explore prosperity, prosperity is not riches. *Prospherah* means to bring, to set before, a sacrifice, gift, or a bestowing of benefits.

Ecclesiastes 11:1 tells us, *Cast your bread upon the waters. For you will find it after many days. Give a serving to seven, and also to eight, for you do not know what evil will be on the earth. If the clouds are full of rain, they empty themselves upon the earth. And if a tree falls to the south or the north, n the place where the tree falls, there it shall lie. He who observes the wind will not sow, and he who regards the clouds will not reap. As you do not know what is the way of the wind, or how the bones grow n the womb of her who is with, so you do not know the works of God who makes everything. In the morning sow your seed, and in the evening do not withhold your hand; for you do not know which will prosper, either this or that, or whether both alike will be good."* Once you have spent it and wasted it there is no going back to get it.

You do not know the way of the wind or how the bones of a child grow in the womb, so you don't know the ways of God. Do not withhold your hand with the morning seed or the evening. If you are scared to give, cast or invest: you can cast it as bread, give it as an offering, or invest it, and then the tree will die.

Chasha means "to be successful"; "to be correctly aligned or positioned" or "to have the necessary requirements." Prosperity from this perspective is to be right. To prosper is to be correctly aligned with the right requirements. Something happens when you invest, you become properly positioned. Prosperity to most people is money: "Give me the money," one might say, "and I will know I am prosperous." You can be prosperous with the right requirements, and there are no limits on requirements. I can give you the money and that is it. If you are correctly positioned, then your favor will last.

You want God to put you in the right place at the right time? I didn't do anything to get here. God just had me at the right place at the right time, and somebody was giving away what I needed. They were retiring and I was getting started, that comes from being properly positioned and that is what God calls prosperous. When you are positioned to receive not something, but everything that God needs for you to get to the next place, this is not to get just a piece of the pie, but this means God will cause someone to drop in your life what is needed to get you to the next place.

God may not give you the million, but he lines you up for it. Remember when Abram gave a tithe to the high priest, and the priest wanted to bless him? Then Abram said, "No, lest you say that you have made me rich." When God gets ready to release favor and the prosperity on you, no man will be able to claim he made you rich. There is an anointing on your offering that goes with the anointing of the tithe, and to give one without the other is to release favor without something to work with. You should stop being afraid of things that challenge you and things that you have never had the chance to do. Many of the challenges you are afraid of are the key to revealing to you who you are and what God wants to produce in your life. Who cares that you have never been in this kind of relationship, you have not had a house note that high or a car note that high? Who cares? With character comes the promise; do no fool around and turn down a promotion because you have never done it before: find out how to do it.

Understand that prosperity is about God aligning you for something that is for a long time. We have had what we thought was prosperity that didn't last. Prosperity lasts, you don't know if it is from what you sowed that morning or what you gave that evening. In the end God says, "Why trip over it? It is vanity, anyway." Get it, tell him "Thank you," and keep on going.

There is an anointing on the offering; prosperity may not be the money, yet it is everything you need with longevity. Give and it shall be given to you, pressed down, shaken together, and running over shall be put into your bosom. Obviously what is put there is not what you have given, where is your bosom? Bosom suggests heart, which is close. Everything God is going to release will be released from the bosom (heart/mind). God said, "Give and

I will turn around and cause you to be right and be properly positioned." Wherever a man's heart is, there his treasure will be also.

The first place prosperity is produced is in the mind and the heart. What stands between many of you and the promises of God is that you have no vision for the promises. God says, "I am not just going to take a whole bunch of stuff and cast it on you." He is going to put it in your mind and pack it real good. Dreams are so important. Just think about some of the wealthiest people in the world, they are dreamers.

You get up every morning and go to work without a clue of the meaning of life, but then one day the anointing on the offering kicks in, and you are face to face with a dream; it blows your mind, it has been there all the time, but you have just never seen it. God wants to press it down, why? Why does he want to shake it together? How can I become a steward of it if it is running over? Obviously God is doing something else. Whatever you dream, you can do it.

Hebrews 7:5 and 8 tells us that the sons of Levi "receive the tithes from the people" and that "mortal men receive tithes, but there he receives them, of whom it is witnessed that he lives." What is this talking about? Mortal men die. There is no record of the death of Melchizedek, who is a type of Christ. So even when mortal men here receive my tithe, there it is received of the one who lives. Even when the ones who receive it are gone, the tithe still lives. God changed the priest in the New Testament so the order had to change. It was working here, but the order because now Christ, who is the high priest, lives forever. We cut out the middle man. When it is received by mortal men, it is witnessed of the one who lives. Tithe no longer operates at a level limited by men. It now has received a supernatural power function order. In his hands it was limited. If we went to battle and failed to give it, it would lose. But in the supernatural function it is working in realms you don't even know and cannot even see, it's what we saw the man of God witness as the tithe was given, and before they would even get a change to fight, their enemies were scattered.

It is of a supernatural function for a supernatural order, and you are giving money that is working supernaturally. What happens when my offering falls under that kind of function? If my tithe is functioning like that, what happens when I release my offering with the tithe? If my offering has supernatural functioning to it, what happens with the rest of the things I have received? Chapter 8 says that Christ is benevolently giving to every man what he needs; tithe is functioning supernaturally. What happens when the minister of the sanctuary gets ready to supply your needs? You can operate without limit, it works through the offering that is holy and supernatural, and your money transcends natural bounds.

You have passed your offering on, and everything else that you possess is connected to the offering that is connected to the tithe. You cannot be any better positioned or more properly aligned. This is the "hook up" of life. You don't get any better connection than Christ. Everything else you possess will prosper.

You want people to start asking, "How do you do what you do?" When they know what they pay you is not enough, give your tithes and offering. There is an anointing on your offering.

BIOGRAPHY

His charismatic style and delivery of God's Word captures the attention of believers worldwide. He translates Orthodox Greek and Hebrew vocabulary into layman's terms, breeding further revelatory insight of scripture for new and seasoned believers. His preaching emanates his innate gift to encourage, empower and inspire every believer, no matter what status of relationship they have with Christ. In Sierra Leone, West Africa he is named *"The Fire Man".*

Born into a lineage of clergy and having accepted Jesus Christ as Lord and Savior very early in life, Bishop Scott began expressing his gift to preach and sing in local congregations as God was modeling him into the servant he is today. Maintaining his commitment to God, by age fifteen he officially accepted his call to preach the gospel. Appointed pastor of his first church, by age 19, Bishop Scott fulfilled his mission to Mt. Zion Baptist Church, a historically black church located in Houston's midtown area. His seven year tenure at Mt. Zion concluded his appointment to pastor the church with a brand new beginning of leadership for a new ministry. Organizing a church from an embryonic stage was new to him. However, this assignment was and still is a mandate for his journey by God. On April 3, 1994, Trinity Fellowship Church was organized, holding its very first service April 10, 1994.

Though criticized and ridiculed, He sought guidance, and divine inspiration from God to establish and execute an apostolic ministry to develop and impact believers who will embrace and commit their gift of apostle, pastor, evangelist, prophet, and teacher for the work of the Kingdom.

Fast-forward ten years after organizing Trinity Fellowship Church, Bishop Scott was consecrated on April 3, 2004 as Bishop under the auspices of Kingdom Fellowship Covenant Ministries, Inc. by the Most Right Reverend Ralph L. Dennis; proven the epitome of a shepherd's heart during his election of Bishop. Bishop Scott had successfully demonstrated the work of equipping men and women for the work of perfecting the saints for the work of ministry, and edifying the body of Christ. Fulfilling his role as an overseer and a spiritual covering, Bishop Scott founded the New Beginnings Fellowship of Pastors and Ministries which consists of several ministries throughout the state of Texas.

As senior pastor of Trinity Fellowship Church, Bishop Scott continuously ministers power packed sermonic teachings to hundreds of parishioners and thousands of internet radio listeners worldwide. His most requested audio series include: "How to Walk In Your Destiny", "How to Touch the Invisible", "Overcoming the Way of the Gentiles", "Closing the Door to Generational Curses and "Covenant Relationship-The Importance of Marriage".

An extraordinary and gifted singer, Bishop Scott's soft, reverential voice tugs the ears and hearts of the audience as he echoes and hums melodic tunes invoking an atmosphere of corporate praise and worship. His surrendering to the Holy Spirit postures him as a conduit for spiritual gifts to flow and operate as he wills – edifying the saints and new converts to another dimension of spiritual maturity.

Bishop Scott has been a featured vocalist with powerhouse national artists and writers such as: Yolanda Adams, Kim Burrell, Marvin Sapp, Shawn McClemore, V. Michael McKay and many more.

Unfailing in his season of labor, this multi-gifted servant, penned two powerfully educating books entitled "True Stewardship" and Tithes and It's Anointing".

Bishop Scott is married to Zandra Denise and together they have five children Garelyn, Bishop, Mecale, Gabrielle, and Gary II.

Printed in the United States
by Baker & Taylor Publisher Services